BRITISH TRUCKS AT WORK

IN THE 'SIXTIES

First published in 1988 by Roundoak
Publishing, Nynehead, Wellington, Somerset
TA21 OBX.

British Library Cataloguing in Publication
Data

Davies, Peter
    1. Trucks—Great Britain—History
    I. Title
    629.2'24

ISBN 1-871565-00-6

Jacket Photograph: Popularly known as a 'Mickey
Mouse', this S21-cabbed Foden eight wheeler is shown
approaching Archway Hill on the main northbound
route out of London. A 1963 model, it ran in the South
East London fleet of A R Holder & Sons Ltd who
operated a trunk service to the East Midlands. The
sturdy front bumper appears to have been transplanted
from a Leyland of the same period. Behind the Foden is
a 1950 AEC Mammoth Major Mk III of Trowbridge
Transport, Sheffield.

Designed by Peter Davies

Reprinted in 2002 by
The Amadeus Press,
Cleckheaton, West Yorkshire

BRITISH TRUCKS AT WORK

IN THE 'SIXTIES

A Pictorial Review of Road Haulage

A 1950 Scammell 'Rigid Eight' of S Harrison & Sons (Transport) Ltd heads down a lonely stretch of the Great North Road near Grantham on a November morning in 1964.

by

Peter Davies

Roundoak Publishing, Nynehead, Wellington, Somerset

An AEC Mammoth Major Mk V pulls into the Longridge yard of J Robinson while a loaded Leyland Octopus 24.O/4 waits to set out on its next trip. This scene captures much of the character of post-war British haulage.

PREFACE

Photographing working trucks is regarded as a somewhat unusual hobby and those who engage in it are often viewed with suspicion. This was even more the case back in the 'fifties and 'sixties. Many an enthusiast faced needless aggression from unsympathetic drivers and security men!

Quite apart from such hazards, truck photography can be an uphill struggle against the unkind hand of fate. For every achievement there are numerous failures.

It is perhaps better not to dwell on missed opportunities but to value the successes. .In this volume I am pleased to share some of those results with you, the reader, in the hope that you will gain enjoyment, as I have done, from a fascinating subject.

During the 'sixties my limited resources restricted me to a cheap camera which had none of today's luxuries. Focusing was entirely a matter of guesswork and exposures too had to be judged without the aid of a light meter. Inevitably some shots suffered technically as a result. It should be borne in mind that many vehicles were shot on the move so there was even less time to think and only one chance to shoot. Because the subject of liveries held so much interest I set out to record as many as I could in colour. These have been shot mainly on Ektachrome which, as a transparency film, gives even less latitude for errors in exposure.

I hope this collection of pictures will impart a side of haulage which is rarely projected - the colour, the ambience and the whole ethos of what is an indispensable part of modern society. The image of the truck has all too often been dented by irrational attacks from politicians and the press.

This book serves as a modest tribute to an industry which has formed the basis of a fascinating hobby. My gratitude goes to the many operators and drivers who have allowed me to photograph their vehicles over the years and my apologies go to those who were unexpectedly 'captured' on film from the roadside.

PETER DAVIES
October 1988

The face of British trucks - this 1956 Foden 'Chinese Six' of J & T Sharrocks Ltd, Rochdale, typifies the traditional livery style of the period. The V-front 'S18' cab is remembered as a true classic.

CONTENTS

Taking a Look at Trucks

They're good to look at. They're good to listen to. They are only machines built to do a job of work, but even grown ups get 'hooked' on them. Trucks, or lorries as they are more correctly called in Britain, have captured the imagination of all age groups since the days of steam wagons. Even the not so mechanically minded can understand the thrill of steam power. Steam wagons, akin to the great railway locomotives, kindled that sense of adventure which underlies any schoolboy's ambition to be a train driver. The rhythmic motion of well oiled machinery has a hypnotic effect, spiced with the anticipation of journeying to far off places. Some of that sense of excitement has survived into the diesel era, and, for over half a century, heavy goods vehicles have continued to fascinate enthusiasts from all walks of life.

Above all it is the appearance of trucks - their well-balanced proportions, their functional simplicity, their richly designed liveries - which appeal to most. Some names of companies and places have a poetry all of their own. Regional tastes add a piquancy to the overall genre.

Lorry signwriting is an art form in its own right, yet many such creations have only one hope of being recorded and that is through the camera. Whilst most works of art are carefully preserved for future generations, those in the form of working trucks have but a short life, frequently ending their days mouldering in scrapyards. It is partly this vulnerability which makes the experience of observing trucks so precious.

The present day transport scene is no less fascinating than the past. It is a scene of

Some names and addresses have a poetic ring to them. These two work-worn stalwarts of the mid 'fifties bear the memorable livery of T W 'Dick' Nightingale whose fleet epitomised British haulage in the 'sixties.

'high-tech' machinery in which turbocharged diesels and aerodynamic styling are very much the order of the day. Today's long haul trucks are just as worthy of the enthusiast's attentions and indeed many hauliers successfully manage to adapt traditional liveries to the modern lines of the ERFs, Volvos, Scanias, and DAFs which now appear on British roads. Others move with the trends, giving us exciting new liveries which will recall the state of the art in the 'eighties.

Radical changes in transport are frequently linked to changes in legislation as society adapts to an ever developing industry on an international scale. It is as if the ultimate goal is a world-wide standard without frontiers. Thankfully, from the enthusiast's viewpoint, that goal is a long way off. The variety of trucks in different countries is still quite wide. Even within Europe there is still a great deal of individuality. The excitement of seeing, at first hand, the indigenous breeds of trucks in their native surroundings is still to be enjoyed. The contrasts in types and liveries was even greater back in the 'sixties.

In Britain two landmarks in transport history stand out - the 1930 Road Traffic Act and the new Construction and Use Regulations of 1964. Coinciding as it did with the arrival of the diesel engine, the 1930 legislation laid the foundations for the modern truck as we know it. Save for minor amendments in 1955 the 1930 Construction and Use laws remained in force well into the motorway age. British transport thus saw three decades of heavy truck production dominated by 'thirties style forward control, diesel-engined 4, 6 and 8 wheelers ranging from 12 to 22/24-tons gross weight.

This unchanging scene was suddenly rocked by the impact of the 1964 leglislation which permitted the use of 32-ton gross articulated vehicles in Britain. It was a revolution which completely changed the character of UK road transport. It was, from the economic angle, a necessary revolution - higher weights and the use of standard shipping containers were vital in improving efficiency. Britain had been in danger of being left behind in the race to co-ordinate international standards.

Britain's motorway era was dawning in the late 'fifties and truck manufacturers

After a hard working life of maybe 12 or 15 years the majority of heavies are condemned to the scrap heap. Although a few dedicated preservationists have saved a handful of worthy trucks in their correct liveries, most will never be seen again.

were beginning to introduce more powerful engines to cope with the higher speeds and increased distances. Also, by the late 'sixties, vehicle maintenance and safety had been increasingly under scrutiny and compulsory plating and testing was introduced, in 1968, with the aim of improving safety standards. The combined effects of motorways, higher gross weights and compulsory testing was tantamount to a nation-wide cull of traditional British lorries. It marked the end of a dynasty which had survived three decades. To many, this had been a very special period in haulage. It saw the birth of the oil-engined

eight wheeler, the formation of many famous fleets, and the peak of achievement for the British truck industry at home and abroad. The late 'forties will be remembered as the era of British Road Services and that of well-engineered lorries from a host of famous manufacturers. From AEC, Albion, Atkinson, Bristol, Dennis, ERF, Foden, Guy, Leyland, Maudslay, Scammell, Seddon, Sentinel and Thornycroft. It was Britain's "Golden Era".

The late 'sixties saw Britain slipping back in its own market. European makers were stealing the limelight - a process which has gained momentum throughout the past 25 years and has left Britain with a much reduced truck industry.

Whilst present day trucks have great appeal for enthusiasts, those of the "Golden Era" had their own special character. In appearance they had a rugged simplicity which was even more pleasing than the lavish styling of today.

In some ways lorries may have changed considerably since the 'thirties, but in other ways they have not. Beneath their glossy skins, current vehicles are remarkably simi-

Many British trucks of the post-war period had a rugged simplicity. Few highlight this more than the short wheelbase eight wheeler. This 1955 Foden tanker hauled caustic soda for the Murgatroyd Salt & Chemical Co.

UK-built Swiss Volvo CH230 at 28 tonnes gvw echoes the perfectly balanced proportions of pre-1964 British eight wheel tippers.

lar to their ancestors. Perhaps the most significant changes have come about in the past 25 years. Fail-safe parking brakes, load-sensitive braking, tubeless tyres and power-assisted controls are now regarded as basic requirements. In principle most components are not that different from those of half a century ago. Semi-elliptic leaf springs, drum brakes, constant-mesh gearboxes, water cooled diesel engines, and worm and nut steering gears are still almost universal. Cabs and in-cab equipment have of course made dramatic advances in recent years. The current trend towards silicon chip technology in controls and warning systems will no doubt bring further revolutionary changes for the driver.

The external appearance of lorries has changed only a gradual pace since 1930. During the 'forties development was held back by World War II. New cab designs did not begin to appear until the late 'forties, replacing 'thirties designs which had carried on after the war. In the 'fifties more attention was being put into styling. Wrap round windscreens and moulded glass-reinforced plastics began to replace the old coachbuilt cabs with their opening windscreens and wood framing. Some heavy vehicle manufacturers who had traditionally built chassis only, began fitting "mass-produced" pressed steel cabs.

There are widely differing opinions as to what constitutes an attractive looking vehicle - sometimes simplicity pays off, other times heavily styled cabs can become classics in their own right. In their eagerness to make their mark, some aspiring designers of the 'fiftes ran amok with styling cliches and their creations could sometimes be described as grotesque. Most European countries were more adventurous than the UK when it came to cab styling - British trucks exported to Europe often had locally built cabs to suit provincial tastes. British designs tended to be too conservative by European standards.

In every country there are memorable trucks which rank as "classics". Rather like wine, trucks mature with time and some are remembered as good vintages. Take the British AEC Mammoth Major MkIII of the early 'fifties. In appearance it was most individualistic but it is remembered as a true thoroughbred. Its peers included the Foden S18, the ERF V-type, the Leyland 600 series and the Sentinel DV.

Other countries have produced great classics too. Take the early 'sixties French Bernard TD15035 and the long-nosed Berliet TLM10M for instance, and Switzerland's famous normal control Saurer 'C' series. From Germany came the bonneted Mercedes Benz L312 and Bussing LS11. Belgium's Gardner-powered Automiesse bonneted tractor is another memorable "classic" of its era.

Advances in design, both mechanical and aesthetic have edged forwards throughout transport history. The pace of advancement

European styling was more adventurous than British. This Belgian Foden FG8/15 was photographed in Antwerp in 1965. Whether or not it rivals the standard British Foden in the beauty stakes is a matter of opinion. The extended 'sleeper' style cab conveniently conceals the long straight-eight Gardner.

has varied, sometimes restrained by economic crises, sometimes spurred on by legislative change or by competition in a tough market.

Although looks might count, overall efficiency is probably the most important quality in trucks. Ever since Gottlieb Daimler coaxed his two- cylinder two-tonner into life over 90 years ago, the search for improved efficiency has been under way. As engineers and designers explore new ideas so the process of evolution continues. Competition in a free market is probably the biggest stimulus

French classic of the late 'fifties was the long nosed Berliet TLM10M. This striking 180bhp machine grossed 35 tonnes gcw and was fitted with the optional sleeper cab for international journeys.

for improvement. Manufacturers are out to score points over their rivals to keep up with the front runners.

Until the late 'fifties and the first motorways British heavy trucks were powered to move a maximum of 22 tons at a modest legal maximum speed of 20mph. Needless to say that by today's standards they were woefully under-powered and uncomfortably slow. Top speed was usually about 30-35 mph at maximum engine speeds of around 1800 revs. Operators did not want more power if it was at additional cost. They wanted minimum weight, minimum fuel consumption and minimum overall cost. It wasn't until the export drive of the late 'forties and early 'fifties that any power increases had been thought necessary. By the mid 'fifties AEC had their AV690 and Leyland their O.680 150 bhp units in full production and Gardner were soon to announce their 6LX in 1957 at the same power rating. Gardner's earlier 8LW launched in 1945 had provided 150 bhp for some applications, notably Foden and Atkinson. But the 8LW was a long 'straight-8' engine and its rear end usually protruded into the body space on rigids. 8LW-powered Atkinsons with their 'fifties coachbuilt cabs took on a most imposing appearance with their wider radiators for added cooling.

It was in the late 'fifties that Cummins arrived on the UK scene to compete with Gardner in the heavy duty diesel engine field. Seddon and ERF were among the first to offer Cummins, namely the HF6, 180 bhp 6-cylinder. Rolls Royce too were becoming more active in the automotive diesel world with their 180 bhp C6NFL. With higher output engines, overdrive 6-speed gearboxes and

higher axle ratios, most leading heavies were now capable of speeds in the upper 50s and longer daily journeys were becoming possible.

Prior to the new Construction and Use Regulations of August 1964 most builders of maximum weight rigids offered short wheelbase chassis for tipper applications and visually these had a special appeal all of their own. Such machines were commonly fitted with high-sided tipping bodies or bulk tanks presenting a very solid workmanlike appearance. In fact there can be few trucks to rival the impression of solid power conveyed by these chunky short wheelbased tippers from Foden, AEC, Albion, Guy, ERF and many others during the 'fifties. To see such ideally balanced proportions nowadays one must go to Switzerland where weight regulations still favour the type. In the UK outer axle spread limitations call for long wheelbase heavy tippers at maximum gross weight.

In the 'sixties the new breed of 32-ton artics were of 5-axle configuration, because of length limits, and a popular arrangement featured the twin steer tractor unit or 'Chinese Six' as they are popularly known. It is a type still seen in Italy but UK legislation in 1972 allowed longer 32-ton artics, on four axles, effectively killing off the 'Chinese Sixes'. During their few years of UK popularity such machines were marketed by AEC in the form of their Ergomatic cabbed Mammoth Minor, by Foden, Atkinson, and ERF. Leyland and Guy also offered them, but very few actually went into service. Many operators who had existing 24-ton rigid eights converted them into 'Chinese Six' tractors to

The Belgian Automiesse - an excellent example of the functional, well-proportioned European trucks of the 'sixties.

take advantage of the higher artic gcw's. In consequence there was quite a variety of "one-offs" in operation, some of which were very striking machines. If anything, the 'Chinese Six' 5-axle artic was the most imposing looking maximum capacity outfit on the roads in its time.

The return of the 5-axle configuration following amendments to the C & U Regulations effective from May 1st 1983, saw the re-emergence of 3-axled units for 38 tons, but because of weight distribution characteristics the extra axle was added at the rear end, sometimes as a liftable non-steering trailing axle and sometimes as a set back steering axle. Double drive, 3-axle units are heavier and therefore less popular except in the case of off-road operations such as tippers and waste disposal vehicles. Rear steering 3-axle tractors have the advantage of lower weight, lower purchase price and lower tyre costs.

Out of the vast and varied array of truck

1964 UK Construction & Use regulations gave birth to a completely new breed of trucks - the 5-axle artics. These were sometimes of the 'Chinese Six' configuration which provided balanced axle loadings. This Cummins-engined LV-cabbed ERF outfit joined the Stoke-on-Trent fleet of Carman's Transport in 1966.

types which have taken to our highways during the past half century of so, some strike an unforgettable chord, where appearance and sound are blended to perfection. Such gems appear throughout recent transport history. A good example was the Foden FE6/15 2-stroke, in short wheelbase tanker form - a type operated by the Murgatroyd Salt & Chemical Co for the transport of caustic soda.

Often if a lorry looks good and sounds good then it is also a good performer, but this is by no means a hard and fast rule. Of course no operator will tolerate poor reliability even if it is from the prettiest and sweetest sounding lorry in creation. Neither do drivers have much sentimentality when it comes to living with trucks. They too are looking for reliability combined with comfort. Quite often the best looking and best sounding vehicles in the enthusiasts' view find no favour with drivers. Some of those chunky, heavily-engineered creations of the 'fifties might delight the eyes and ears of enthusiasts but drivers would readily complain of poor vision, heavy steering, draughty cabs and deafening engine noise.

Perhaps the truck to satisfy everyone has not yet been designed but to those who just enjoy watching them and listening to them there are many favourites in the post war period. The immense variety of types must

Old rigid eights were often converted into 'chinese six' tractor units. This one is believed to have started life as a petrol tanker.

certainly hold some interest for even the casual bystander and every region of the UK has its memorable classics especially from the 'fifties and 'sixties. Enthusiasm towards the subject of road haulage seems to be growing and interesting new vehicles continue to appear. Future trends are, as always at the mercy of legislation, so it is difficult to predict too far ahead with any accuracy.

Environmental pressures are often at odds with economic ideals. Weight-saving achieved by careful design and the use of newly developed materials can be cancelled out by the compulsory fitment of additional equipment to meet some new legal requirement.

Even as this book goes to press there are legislative changes just 'around the corner' which will affect the appearance of future trucks. For instance, safety legislation which called for rear under-run bumpers and compulsory sideguards may be extended to include front under-run protection. Increased use of fairings, spoilers and deflectors to cut down wind drag is having a big impact on vehicle appearance. Legislation is also being aimed at reducing noise outputs.

Throughout automotive history there have been bold departures from conventional design. We have seen many innovations like battery-electric power, petrol electrics, gas turbines and the highly developed Doble steamers. Similarly there were new ideas on lightweight integral construction like those from Jensen and Mann Egerton. Such principles may well re-emerge some time in the future.

Enthusiasts can look foward to interesting developments in the future and enjoy, perhaps even more so, memories of the past. The pictures in this book recall some of the haulage vehicles seen on British roads during the rapidly changing 'sixties.

Representing current trends in truck design - a 38 ton gcw, 6-axle Leyland-DAF FTG 95-310 ATI artic. Cab design is shared with Seddon Atkinson and Pegaso.

The Regions

For convenience the contents of this book are dealt with on a regional basis roughly corresponding to the Traffic Areas responsible for the licencing of Road Transport in Great Britain. This map shows the approximate boundaries of those areas. In some cases adjacent areas have been combined.

The country is divided up into eleven traffic areas. The Scottish area is sub-divided into two. For the purposes of this book, the Metropolitan and South Eastern areas have been combined, as have the South Wales and Western areas. West Midlands, East Midlands and Eastern areas have likewise been dealt with under one section.

Some county boundaries were changed in the early seventies so references might relate to counties as they were in the sixties.

It is worth noting that the Traffic Area boundaries do not necessarily correspond to county boundaries. Some brief explanation of the extent of each area has been included in each of the following sections. It is by no means definitive and is meant only as a rough guide.

Among the most memorable of British trucks were the Mk III AECs built from 1948 to 1958. While cab styles varied the tall protruding radiator remained instantly recognisable. This 1951 eight wheeler of Cardiff-based Dixon Bool was one of many in service with South Wales operators of the period.

Opposite: Captured in its original dark blue livery is this 'tin-front' AEC Mk III at a time when its operators, Wincanton Transport & Engineering, were repainting their large milk tanker fleet in 'Unigate' orange. This vehicle, fleet name 'Redwing' dates from 1957 and was photographed at their Wincanton headquarters.

South Wales and the West

One immediately links certain commodities with certain places. Think of steel, for instance, and South Wales springs to mind. In a similar way china clay is immediately linked with Cornwall. These are among the leading products which account for much of the traffic in the South Western region.

The British Steel Corporation, formed under the Labour Government in 1967, dominates the industrial scene in parts of South Wales. Before nationalisation the prominent producers were the Steel Company of Wales Ltd based in Port Talbot, and Richard Thomas & Baldwins at Ebbw Vale, Llanwern, near Newport, and Pontypool. The Steel Company of Wales' huge fleet of Albion and Leyland eight wheelers were a fine sight in their green livery with white roofs and red headboards. The trucks were operated by a wholly owned subsidiary called Monmouthshire Transport.

Among the other memorable names were Blue Line Transport, John Raymond and Vale Transport, all based at Bridgend. Also Newport Haulage Services with their smart ERFs and Leylands in cream and green, Abernant Transport, Entress Transport and Hills Transport (Dinas Powis).

British Road Services, of course, handled a large share of the steel transport, running regular services to the Midlands and London.

The transport of coal and chemicals and their many by-products also feature significantly in the industrial regions of South Wales. British Hydrocarbon Chemicals Ltd at Port Talbot had smart blue AEC Mk V tankers on hire from James Hemphill of Glasgow. Also Bulwark Transport operated eight wheel tankers on this contract.

One material which is to be found in abundance in the South West is china clay. The source of this widely used material is The English China Clay Co at St. Austell.

The cosmetic, paper and pottery industries are among the main users and the precious white powder forms

the bulk of return loads for trucks running to the South West. Subsidiary ECC companies in the 'sixties were Heavy Transport (ECC) Ltd, Western Express Haulage (ECC) Ltd and Glover and Uglow Ltd.

Much West Country traffic consists of perishables - meat and eggs from Devon, fish from Cornwall, milk and dairy produce from Somerset. Two of the largest operators who built up their business mainly on milk transport originate from the rural areas of Somerset and Wiltshire. One is Wincanton Transport & Engineering Co who were founded in 1925 and operated a large AEC fleet in the 'sixties. The other is Bulwark Transport of Chippenham.

Among the other vehicles regularly seen in the South West were the AEC tippers of Frank Tucker of Heavitree, Exeter in their cream and brown 'Westbrick' livery. Then there were Western Transport's AECs from their large fleet based in Bristol. Further north at Stroud is the beautifully kept tipper fleet of Moreton C Cullimore.

Chipping Sodbury on the outskirts of Bristol was the home of R & W Febry's fleet, largely Leyland in the 'sixties.

Bristol with its busy Avonmouth Docks was another interesting centre for the truck enthusiast. It was also the home of Bristol Commercial Vehicles, which under the control of the British Transport Commission, developed and built the famous 'HG6L' and 'HA6' trucks for British Road Services.

The only other West Country truck builder was Rowe Hillmaster who offered a wide range of vehicles from 1953 to 1962.

There are numerous other well known own-account fleets and hauliers which are worthy of mention, such as Harris Bacon with their Calne-based Leylands, G F Lovell & Co Ltd of Newport with their superb Atkinson eight wheel box vans liveried "Lovell's Toffee Rex".

Many of the firms mentioned are, of course, still in operation. The following picture round up will perhaps recapture some of the famous names of the 'sixties.

By the late 'sixties when this photograph was taken Guy Vixens were already becoming quite a rarity. These 4-tonners, powered by a 3.7 litre 60bhp 4-cylinder OHV petrol engine, were a quality-built lightweight competing in the weight class normally dominated by mass produced trucks. This 1958 example was one of 4 employed by Tappers of Truro on fruit delivery in Cornwall. A Perkins P4 diesel engine was also available.

Spiers Road Services of Melksham, Wiltshire were well known for their smart fleet of dark brown AECs and have even kept AECs running to this day even though the marque ceased in the late 'seventies. This 1955 'tin-front' Mk III was photographed in London in 1964.

One of the largest and best known bulk liquid haulage fleets in the country was Bulwark Transport with their headquarters in Chippenham. This old established company is part of the United Transport Group. Many of their vehicles were in contract liveries of famous customers. This 1964 Atkinson L2486 beer tanker is seen in their period livery of green when photographed at a Birmingham brewery in the late 'sixties.

A lesser known make of truck was the Rowe Hillmaster built by M G Rowe at Liskeard, Cornwall. During their nine-year period of manufacture a considerable range of chassis was offered covering four wheelers, six wheelers and tractor units. Choice of engines included Perkins, AEC, Gardner, Leyland and Meadows. This 1958 LM/7 with demountable livestock container was photographed at Liskeard in 1969.

Based on the westernmost part of the Cornish peninsular this AEC Mammoth Major TG8R belonged to Suttons of Newlyn, Penzance who specialise in the transport of fresh fish from the Cornish ports to London markets. Eight wheelers were chosen partly for the additional safety offered by the second axle in the event of a front tyre blow-out. With its 187bhp 'AV691' the TG8R had greater power than most of the competition and was the best choice to cope with the demanding Cornish hills. Some of Suttons' later TG8Rs had the even bigger 'AV760' at 206bhp. One still might wonder how they would perform alongside Suttons' current Foden 8-wheelers with more than 300bhp on tap.

One company noted for its excellent livery and the use of fleet names is Moreton C Cullimore, tipper operators based at Stroud in Gloucestershire. Fodens predominated in their fleet, this example being an S21 'Mickey Mouse' six wheeler of 1962.

Entress Transport of Swansea had a considerable eight wheeler fleet featuring Leyland, Atkinson and AEC engaged on general haulage. They operated a regular London trunk using numerous ex British Road Services vehicles. This Leyland Octopus 22.O/1 formerly 2OG554 with BRS was photographed at the Entress yard in 1966.

Read is a name synonymous with haulage in Gloucestershire. Brothers Richard, Harold, George, Ivor, Fred & David all operated trucks. This 1966 Atkinson S2486X tipper was operated by Richard Read from his Longhope base in the Forest of Dean. Ivor Read ran tippers and Fred Read's fleet was based at Ross-on-Wye. Oldest of the brothers, David, had a fleet of lorries on coal delivery in Oldham. Their father John was in the haulage business too, in Hereford, back in the days of steam traction engines.

One of the most important Cornish products is china clay used in a wide range of industries from pottery and paper to pharmaceuticals and cosmetics. The English China Clay Group's local transport fleet operates under the name Heavy Transport Co. and is based at St. Austell. This scene at the company's Port of Par shows bulk supplies of the fine white powdered clay being loaded directly on to a ship. The 24 ton gross Foden 'S20' and the Leyland 24.O/5 eight wheeled tippers date from the mid 'fifties.

Two smart tilt-cabbed Albion Super Reivers operated on long distance general haulage by W J Rich & Sons of Crediton, Devon. These were the last type of Albion marketed before British Leyland chose to discontinue the marque in 1972. From then on they featured the Bathgate 'G' cab common with the BMC Redline range. Albions were rather ignominiously dubbed the 400 range. Both BMC and Albion carried the Leyland name badge.

Making its steady, plodding way along the A40 trunk road towards London, this 1954 Atkinson L1266 was one of a fleet operated by H Pye and Son's subsidiary, Co-ordinated Contracts for British Nylon Spinners who were based at Panteg, near Pontypool. Most of the fleet were fitted with integral van bodies featuring a distinctive 'domed' luton head. Of the 178 vehicles and 200 semi trailers, twenty or so were Atkinson six wheelers. The other vehicles were specially designed close-coupled artics with Bedford tractor units and Carrimore trailers.

Albion Motors joined the Leyland Group in 1951. The LAD (Leyland Albion Dodge) cab became standard in the late 'fifties. This Reiver tipper of J Maggs dates from 1964.

Seen against a back drop of Cornwall's 'Pyramids' is a Bedford KM tipper belonging to English China Clay subsidiary Glover & Uglow. Parts of the Cornish landscape were once dominated by these huge peaks of waste material from the clay workings. This 1968 KMR was powered by the 143 bhp, 466 cu in Bedford diesel engine.

George Read's fleet at Micheldean was acquired by British Road Services Ltd in 1965. This rather unusual Albion HD53 went 'full circle' since it had been purchased ex-BRS only a few years earlier. Originally a lwb 4- wheeler, Read's had it converted to a tractor unit. It operated for much of its time in Newport transporting steel coils from RTB's Spencer Works to the docks. Many late 'HDs' were designated HD73 and were powered by the Leyland O.600. This circa 1953 version had the Albion EN253 engine.

The newly formed Forest of Dean branch of British Road Services also acquired James Smith of English Bicknor whose fleet was relocated at Mitcheldean. Prior to that vehicles were finished in a smart green livery with gold lettering. This 24.O/4 Octopus has the type of low sided dropside body frequently used on steel haulage.

Built solely for British Road Services use Bristol trucks were intended to combine all the best features into one design. Conceived and developed before the 1964 Regulations, Bristol artics like the 1963 HA6G shown here, were soon outmoded. Further development was shelved. One notable feature is the exceptionally large window area of the Longwell Green GRP cab. In total 650 Bristol tractor units were built and 854 ST semi-trailers.

The majority of South Wales haulage companies opted for rigids on long distance work in the early 'sixties. By the late 'sixties the traditional rigid eight with 24ft 6in (7.5m) body was dwindling as new 32-ton artics were bought for economic reasons. Typical of the old-style trucks is this fine S20-cabbed Foden dating from about 1959. The personalised registration number must be nearly 50 years older!

Corona Soft Drinks were the operators of this 1952 ERF 5.6TS twin-steer 'Chinese Six' - a type they favoured for distribution work. At 16 tons gvw, the type was outmoded in the mid 'sixties by new 16-ton four wheelers with 10-ton rear axles and 6-ton front axles.

One of Bulwark Transport's many customers was Richard Thomas & Baldwins in whose livery these two Atkinson L2486 flats appear, hauling steel into the Luton factory of Vauxhall Motors in the early 'sixties.

After the steel industry was nationalised in the late 'sixties the various producers came under the British Steel Corporation, whose standard vehicle livery was a mid-blue. This 1969 Atkinson 'Silver Knight' rear-steer was one of 30 tractors and 60 trailers based at the former Steel Company of Wales' Orb Works, Newport. This vehicle powered by a 220 'Rolls' with a ZF transmission was photographed when new and, although it bears the BSC insignia, it was finished in the mid-green of Monmouthshire Transport Co, referred to on page 29.

Kelly's from Abergavenny were the operators of this 1965 Guy Invincible, one of the last of its type. A remarkably modern concept in truck design when introduced in 1958, they were offered with a choice of Gardner or Leyland engines. The Guy factory, at Fallings Park, Wolverhampton ceased building trucks in the late 'seventies.

In the 'sixties one would see the occasional Vulcan like this 1951 6PF still working. This one was operated by W O Jones, timber merchants, of Tawe Sawmills, Llansamlet, near Swansea. These ruggedly built 6-tonners were powered by a Perkins P6 70bhp diesel and were built at Maidstone in Kent. Production ceased in 1952.

Seen weighing out after unloading sheet steel at Luton is this 1953 AEC Mammoth Major Mk III trailing axle eight wheeler, one of a huge fleet of rigid eights based at BRS Cardiff. By the end of the 'sixties virtually all these long serving veterans had vanished as articulated vehicles were brought in to replace them.

Like the Bristol artic on p23, Bristol HG6L eight wheelers were built exclusively for British Road Services. All were designed and manufactured by the Bristol Tramways & Carriage Co which was acquired when the Tilling Group was nationalised. 517 HG6Ls were built between 1952 and 1957. This one bears chassis no. 132010. It was built in 1957 by which time the company had been renamed Bristol Commercial Vehicles. Leyland O.600 diesel engines were fitted in all the rigid eights.

Styling which might have been considered bold by British standards made the bonneted Leyland Comet stand out from the crowd when it was launched in 1948. Originally aimed at the overseas market these striking vehicles became very popular throughout the UK. The later models were powered by the 100bhp Leyland O.350 diesel and were in production until 1959. This 1955 example was photographed near Port Talbot and belonged to haulage contractor H Griffiths.

Monmouthshire Transport Co, a subsidiary of the Steel Company of Wales continued to operate Albion eight wheelers until they ceased to be available in 1960. This policy carried over from the company's pre-nationalisation connections with the United Transport Group. The Caledonian shown here dates from 1957 and despite being similar in appearance to the contemporary Leyland Octopus, differs in all but the cab, engine and gearbox.

Gwynne Bowen's trucks were noted for their excellent colour scheme and gold leaf signwriting. During the 'fifties they ran a large fleet of Foden, Atkinson, ERF,

AEC and Thornycroft eight wheelers on long distance trunk services to Lancashire and the north. This 1959 Albion Reiver was photographed at their Gorseinon headquarters.

J M Watkins of Abergavenny operated this 1959 KV-cabbed ERF 6.8G. The KV Cab, introduced in 1954, was a modern concept featuring wide wrap-round windscreens and a stylish oval grille. It stood the test of time well and although replaced by the LV in 1962 it still looks modern to this day.

Full ahead on the A40 trunk route - a 1958 Atkinson L2486 from the fleet of Ross Garages, Cardiff. Ross were Atkinson agents in the South Wales area and their dark green trucks were a familiar sight in most parts of Great Britain. Fleet strength in the 'sixties was around 50 and regular trunk services were operated mainly to Sheffield and London.

Penarth Road, Cardiff was the headquarters of Hills Transport (Dinas Powis) Ltd whose large fleet included maximum capacity eight wheeled rigids like this 1960 AEC G8RA Mk V flat. They were engaged on general haulage. Loads included steel, building materials and foodstuffs. A regular trunk was operated to London and Manchester.

From the rural region of central Wales this 1960 Albion Reiver, owned by Tregaron-based J D James, was operated on regular runs to Liverpool and London taking butter and milk powder from the local creameries and returning with animal feeding stuffs. It was powered by an O.375 Leyland diesel which was regularly pushed to its outer limits by the demanding roads and steep hills around its home base.

Atkinson rigid eights had the in-built reserves of strength and reliability which suited them to the tough conditions encountered on South Wales steel traffic. Trevor Phillips from Cadoxton, Neath were among the many users of the marque. This 1958 example is in for an easy homeward journey with a load of returnable empty stillages.

Fforestfach on the outskirts of Swansea was the home of haulage contractor Philip Jones whose eight wheeler fleet included AEC, Atkinson and Leyland flats. This 24.O/4 Octopus is a 1957 model with the late 600 series cab.

The functional frontal appearance of British trucks in the post-war era is summed up in this shot of an Albion HD57 belonging to Edwards Transport of Lydbrook, Gloucestershire. With its 9.9 litre engine the HD57 was among the more powerful trucks in its class. Compared with the slow but sure performance of the Gardner 6LW, the Albion EN253 engine had a sprightly turn of acceleration and its controls were unusually light to operate.

KV-cabbed ERF of 1959 vintage in operation with Aberdare Cables Ltd. The 6.8GX model was powered by the 150bhp Gardner 6LX and featured the later version KV cab with four headlamp system and added cooling area on the grille.

Dating from 1953 this 22.O/1 Leyland Octopus flat of Hereford based A G Griffiths & Sons (Transport) Ltd waits in the queue at Vauxhall Motors' AC steel stores in 1965. This model was one of the most successful rigid eights of its day. Its 9.8 litre O.600 diesel developed 125bhp.

Tower Bridge, one of Great Britain's most famous landmarks forms an imposing backdrop to this 1960 Foden FG6/24 which was one of a large fleet of bulk granulated sugar tankers operated by Tate & Lyle from Silvertown. Net payload was 14 tons and the load was discharged pneumatically. The special tank bodies, built by the Airscrew Co & Jicwood tipped to 45 degrees for both loading and unloading.

Opposite: The familiar red AEC Mammoth Major Mk IIIs of Northfleet-based Bowater UK Paper Co were a regular sight around London, meeting the huge demand for newsprint to keep the presses rolling. Bowaters association with AECs went right back to the early 'thirties. Their trucks were always smart and well maintained. This 1951 model was photographed in Borough High Street.

London and the South East

Each part of the country tends to have its own image - an image reflecting dominant facets of its character. The South East conveys an image of affluence and cosmopolitan fashion, far removed from the sweat and grime of heavy industry. Nevertheless it is richly endowed with trucks.

This is not so surprising if you consider the scale of London and its status in international trade. Just the daily demands for food supplies, fuel and consumer goods generates enormous traffic, from the movement of raw materials to the distribution of finished products. When this is combined with the transport requirements for the rest of the area where a host of industries exists, ranging from cement to paper and from motor cars to chemicals, it is easy to see why the South East is the busiest area of all for trucks.

Most major trunk routes radiate from London and long distance traffic converges on the city from all over the country. In the 'sixties when the Motorway system was still confined to a few disjointed sections, the old arterial routes were crammed with slow moving traffic at peak times. The only lucky people were the truck enthusiasts who could enjoy the interminable roar of Gardners and AECs advancing a few yards at a time through a haze of exhaust smoke. Such vantage points for 'lorry spotting' were Archway Road and Barnet High Street, both of which were steady gradients. St Albans was another famous bottleneck where the A6 joined the A5.

Most leading hauliers had London depots, frequently located under railway arches around the Bermondsey area. The Port of London's huge Docklands were still operational in the 'sixties. They extended from Tilbury right up to the Pool of London where St Katherines Dock stood, overlooked by the famous Tower Bridge. Once a busy river crossing for trucks, Tower Bridge was closed to heavy vehicles in 1979 and the whole area has been re-developed, robbing much of the drama from London's unique riverside architecture.

As well as the many hauliers, own-account fleets abounded in

London. These were operated by the larger breweries like Courage, Whitbread and Trumans, and the flour mills including Joseph Ranks, Spillers, Hovis and French's. Perhaps one of the best known fleets was that of Tate & Lyle Transport which originated as Pease Transport. Their magnificent dark blue Foden tankers and AEC eight wheeled flats were a regular sight. Equally impressive was the Silver Roadways fleet which also operated for Tate & Lyle out of its base in Bermondsey Wall West. From Northfleet in Kent, Bowaters' AEC Mammoth Majors were daily visitors to the capital.

The Metropolitan traffic area takes in more than just London of course - it covers Hertfordshire; parts of Surrey; part of South Bedfordshire including Luton and Dunstable; part of Buckinghamshire including Amersham, High Wycombe and Slough; parts of South west Essex, West Kent and North Sussex. The remainder of Kent and Sussex lie in the South Eastern area together with Berkshire, Hampshire the Isle of Wight and parts of South East Dorset and South West Surrey.

The South East was not only one of the best areas for seeing trucks at work, but, surprisingly, it also boasted the largest number of truck manufacturers in the early post-war era. No less than 11 makes - Bedford, Commer and Karrier in the Luton area; AEC at Southall; Scammell at Watford; Dennis at Guildford; Ford at Dagenham and Langley; Dodge at Kew; Vulcan at Maidstone; Thornycroft at Basingstoke and the lesser known Rutland in Croydon.

Two more celebrated own account operators still dominant in the area were the Cement Marketing Company and Tunnel Cement (now called Castle Cement).

There were of course countless other major fleets in the area like Crow Carrying Company, Thomas Allen, Union Cartage, Reed of Aylesford, St Albans Sand and Gravel and Bakers of Southampton, all of whom are worthy of wider mention. The pictures on the following pages feature many more famous names. Perhaps pictures speak louder than words.

An elderly Atkinson still giving service with the large fleet of the North Thames Gas Board in the mid 'sixties. This M1266 tanker bears a 1951 registration mark and was used to transport coal tar mainly for road re-surfacing.

Latter day Thornycroft belonging to Merralls Transport Ltd of Egham, Surrey. This 1961 MHQR6 Mastiff six wheeler was built towards the end of Thornycroft's period in civilian on-road haulage vehicles. In 1961 they became part of Associated Commercial Vehicles (ACV) formed by AEC, Maudslay and Crossley. Thornycroft were then to concentrate on special heavy tractors and crash tenders leaving haulage vehicle build to AEC.

At the lighter end of the truck world this 1958 Dennis Pax III proved a popular choice for beer transport. Luton-based Flowers Brewery, formerly J W Greens, operated this low-load example on local urban distribution of its bottled beers. Soon the pale yellow Flowers trucks were to disappear as they were re-liveried in the Whitbread brown of their parent company. Power for the Pax III came from a Perkins P6, 83bhp diesel and the payload was 6 tons.

One of the most impressive fleets in the Slough area was that of Starch Products who were an own-account operator with flats and bulkers to distribute their products which included adhesives. Best known for their AECs they also operated Fodens and Vulcans. This 1951 FG6/15 eight wheeler was photographed while waiting to load up at their Langley factory in the late 'sixties.

From the late 'thirties onwards the United Molasses Co Ltd operated a distinctive fleet of Scammell Rigid Eight tankers based in London and Liverpool. This one dates from 1957.

The brown trucks of London-based Alfred Dexter were employed on regular London to Liverpool trunk services largely on fruit transport. This 1956 Atkinson T746 artic was seen crossing the famous Tower Bridge, once a busy truck route but since 1979 has been closed to heavy vehicles.

Noted for their 'personalised' registration numbers the Fodens and AECs of Alan Firmin Transport Ltd from Linton in Kent operated on general haulage throughout the country. AF66, an S18-cabbed eight wheeler, was a typical example seen here on the southern end of the M1 motorway. Note the absence of Armco barriers and lamp standards and the lightness of the traffic. AF numbers were originally issued in Cornwall in the 'twenties.

A transport company renowned for its smart fleet of AEC tankers was A E Evans, Regent Transport, from Dagenham. They were among the last operators to run Mk IIIs, many of which were purchased secondhand from the large petrol companies. The vehicle shown dates from 1950.

Dagenham is also the setting for this rather unusual looking Albion Caledonian 4000-gallon petrol tanker operated by Kingsford Haulage. Instead of its standard Leyland '600' series cab it has a special Miles cab with forward sloping screen pillars. It was one of a batch originally built for Shell Mex & BP Ltd in 1959.

Albion Sugar Co tankers featured memorable styling. Built in the 'fifties and early 'sixties on a mixture of S18 and S20 cabbed Foden FGs, their handsome appearance set them apart from other trucks. They carried brewing sugars and syrups for industry and the superb bodywork was built by W P Butterfield of Shipley in Yorkshire. This one, Fleet No 54 was supplied in 1961.

In the 'sixties one could not go far in London's East End without seeing the beautifully-liveried Foden FG6/15 flats of Ranks Flour. The deep body raves were a feature as was the fitment of alkaline batteries. The fleet operated under the name B I Transport Co Ltd.

Apart from the ubiquitous Scammell Highwayman it was unusual to see normal-control or 'conventional' tractor units used on haulage in the UK. Annis & Co from Hayes, Middlesex were noted for their unorthodox trucks. This overseas type AEC Mogul hitched to a Scammell 'frameless' tank trailer is no exception. It dates from 1966 and had a 35-ton gcw design weight. Net power output from the AV760, 12.47 litre engine was 206bhp.

The Scammell Highwayman articulated eight wheeled tanker was one of the most successful vehicles for the transport of bulk liquids. The ultimate evolution of Scammell's original early-twenties design, the latter-day Highwayman III was powered by a Leyland O.680, 200bhp diesel and grossed 32 tons. This 1962 version would still have grossed at 24 tons with the 161bhp O.680 engine. Unlike normal artics the original Scammells were left coupled up and did not even have landing legs. They were simply called 'Eight Wheelers' and were conceived by Scammell as single vehicles.

The distinctive skirted bodies of the Cement Marketing Co flats were immortalised in miniature by Dinky Toys in the form of their Blue Circle Leyland Comet, No. 533. This photograph records the real thing. NUW252, Fleet No. 1039, dates from 1953 and was based at the large Houghton Regis cement works near Dunstable in the 'sixties.

The Packhorse Garage Depot of J & H Transport (Peckham) Ltd, on Watling Street is the setting for this shot of a 1964 Scammell Handyman. The tractor is about to be uncoupled from its tidily sheeted trailer. J & H Transport had a fine fleet of Scammells, Leylands and AECs with depots all over the country. The Handyman shown is the less familiar type built prior to the heavily-styled Michelotti version which appeared in 1965.

An interesting comparison between the standard Scammell ballast tractor used by the Union Cartage Co and its own purpose-built Union tractor which was a rare machine by any standards. A number of these ballasted drawbar tractors were built from a selection of proprietary components. Gardner engines were used and some were fitted with radiators from Foden DGs. They were mainly employed on hauling insulated meat trailers from the docks to the meat market at Smithfield.

The red and blue trucks of Convoys Ltd were a familiar sight around the Fleet Street area, once the centre of the newspaper industry. This 1964 Albion Chieftain 'Super Six' artic carried a payload of 12 tons and was only 7ft 6in (2.3m) wide making it more manoeuvrable in tight corners.

From the large fleet of Victory Transport, Southampton, this 1961 Albion Caledonian flat was engaged on long distance general haulage. Victory Transport, who had a fleet of about 150 trucks and extensive warehousing facilities became a subsidiary of Amey Group Transport, Oxford around 1970.

The Crow Carrying Co, who were based at Barking in Essex before moving to Silvertown in the late 'sixties, were renowned for their huge Scammell fleet which was well kept and nicely liveried in dark blue and black. Crow are members of the Transport Development Group. This shot of a typical 1954 ART.8 oil tanker captures the unique flavour of the period. Dedicated transport men mourn the loss of Scammell which was a pillar of the UK truck industry. The plant was finally closed in 1988.

Among the Leaders in the development of UK/European transport operations of the 'sixties were Lep Transport with their headquarters in East London. 'Ergomatic'-cabbed AEC Mandators like this were more compatible with the European style tandem axle tilt trailers which were still relatively new by British standards.

Few instances have occurred in Great Britain where operators have used load carrying tractor units to haul semi trailers. This type of combination is more common in certain overseas territories and is sometimes referred to as the 'dromedary' outfit. Spurlings, however, for their salt carrying contract with ICI Ltd employed an Atkinson TS3266 Silver Knight 'Chinese Six' tractor unit mounted with a single 7-ton capacity Interconsult 'bubble' tank and fifth wheel on to which was coupled a 'double bubble' semi making an impressive and well balanced combination.

A more conventional configuration was chosen for this Tyburn Road Tank Services artic hauled by a rear-steer 3-axle Atkinson Silver Knight tractor. The maroon Atkinsons of Tyburn were a common sight until the late 'sixties when they adopted the livery of parent company Stephenson Clarke in the Powell Duffryn Group.

An interesting practice which periodically emerges in the UK is the modification of chassis to vary payload capacity and axle weight distribution to suit specific operations. In the 'sixties the Regent Oil Co ran a number of Guy Warriors and AEC Mercurys with 'rear steer' conversions on fuel distribution.

An Atkinson L1586 of E A Smith, Parkfield Garage & Transport Co, Wolverhampton off-loads steel coils assisted by a Coles mobile crane. Within a few years of this truck entering service it was rendered obsolete by the 1964 legislation.

Opposite: Crossing a narrow bridge over the Trent on the Staffordshire border - a 1954 Leyland Octopus with a full load from the London Brick Co at Yaxley. These and AEC Mk IIIs formed the backbone of the huge LBC fleet.

The Midlands and East Anglia

So diverse are the operations found in this region it should come as no surprise that chalk and cheese can be listed among its indigenous commodities.

The East Midlands covers a very large area extending from South West Bedfordshire right up to the border of Yorkshire, and takes in most of Northamptonshire, Leicestershire, Nottinghamshire, and a large part of Derbyshire and Lincolnshire. At its southernmost end it includes Oxfordshire and West Buckinghamshire.

One of the largest operators in the Nottingham area is old established A R Marshall and Sons (Bulwell) Ltd. Then there were the familiar dark blue Fodens of J Watts and the Foden tipper fleet of K & M (Hauliers) Ltd. Nearby Mansfield was the home of Coal Deliveries (E Midlands) some of whose brown eight wheel tippers were rare 'TVWs' built or converted by North Cheshire Motors.

Leicestershire is tipper country with its numerous quarries like Mountsorrel and Bardon. Among the best known haulage fleets were Federated Road Transport Services at Market Harborough whose dark green AECs and Atkinsons formed part of a 100-strong fleet.

Murphy Bros had another impressive fleet of Foden, AEC and Leyland eight wheelers operating out of Thurmaston. Yet another in the 'big league' were A M Walker Ltd of Cosby.

Amongst the notable Derbyshire firms were F B Atkins with their distinctive brown Fodens and wire manufacturers Richard Johnson & Nephew.

Tipper fleets of note included those of Breedon and Cloud Hill Lime Works, W H Phillips of Wirksworth and the unmistakable blue Fodens of Barlow & Hodgkinson at Buxton.

Leighton Buzzard in the southernmost tip of the area has been the base for some well known large fleets. H G Pentus Brown had a considerable fleet of Fodens, AECs and Leylands. Among the other big companies were Frederick Ray Ltd and A E H Dawson.

Moving east, one of Bedfordshire's largest own account fleets was that of the London Brick Company. In the 'sixties the LBC fleet was predominantly AEC and Leyland. Nearby, at Ridgmont, the Marston Valley Brick Co had a large fleet of orange AECs, Fodens and ERFs. They were taken over by LBC in the late 'sixties.

The Eastern area includes a lot of rural territory and most transport fleets are centred around the cities and towns. One of the largest was the Pointer Group of Norwich which also owned Hamblin Haulage of Leicester. Wyatts of Diss - 'Fridged Freight' - had a memorable fleet of fridge outfits mainly of AEC origin. Well known in the Cambridge area are Turners of Soham, Knowles of Wimblington and Welch's of Stapleford.

Lincolnshire had some big named fleets in the northern sector which is officially in the East Midlands area. McVeigh Transport of Grimsby was one. Then there was Humber Warehousing who eventually took over McVeighs.

This area also encompasses industrial towns like Scunthorpe on South Humberside, a large steel producing centre where the distinctive BRS Leyland Octopus fleet with their special long-load dollies were based.

In the West Midlands, Birmingham, Britain's 'second city', is the centre of the motor component industry. Well known hauliers include Chambers & Cook Ltd, Henry Joyner Ltd, Millichamp Haulage Ltd and E & J Davis. Likewise, Wolverhampton and Darlaston are great areas for haulage fleets, among them A T Hartshorne, Parkfield Garage and Transport Co and S Jones (Aldridge) Ltd.

Equally well endowed with trucks - perhaps best of all - is Stoke-on-Trent, which is the base for such celebrated firms as H Tideswell of Kingsley, Bassetts Roadways of Tittensor, Beresfords Transport of Tunstall and Shirleys of Cellarhead. At least some of these legendary companies are illustrated in the following pages.

With its small 2.72 litre two-stroke engine the Foden
FE4/8 was an exceptionally light machine for a full 8-ton
payload. It first appeared in 1953 marking Foden's move
into the 4-cylinder two-stroke field. The FD4 engine
developed 84bhp at 2000rpm. The larger FD6, still only
of 4.1 litres capacity, put out 126bhp. This tipper
belonging to Thomas Burton of Market Harborough was
photographed in Liverpool in 1964.

Tower Hill Transport Co, the trading name of Boston
Stevedores Ltd, were not from London as their name
suggests but from Boston in Lincolnshire. They
operated 148 vehicles from nine depots. Soon after this
1959 24.O/4 Octopus was photographed the company
was to go into receivership. It became Larrow Transport
and was eventually sold off, three of the nine depots
being taken over by the large Davis Bros. organisation.

Murphy Brothers (Transport Division) Ltd of Thurmaston near Leicester ran a number of these AEC Mammoth Major Mk V eight wheelers in their large fleet. Regular trunk services were operated to Liverpool and to South Wales, together with general haulage throughout the UK. This Mk V curiously bears a 1968 registration although production ceased in 1965.

The beautifully liveried Fodens of Richard Johnson & Nephew were a delight to any transport enthusiast passing their Ambergate Works near Derby. This S20-cabbed FG is being sheeted and roped ready for its next trip. Across the back of the cab is written 'The wise buyer buys Johnson's wire'.

An LV-cabbed ERF eight wheeled bulker from the Cromford-based fleet of Midland Storage. This vehicle dating from 1964 was photographed heading north on the A5 trunk road before the completion of the M6 motorway.

This 1966 Seddon 16-4-505 bearing a Derby fleet number was one of approximately fifty built for British Road Services. It was powered by an AEC engine as fitted to the Mercury range. The 6-ton front axle is set back to achieve correct weight distribution.

H Tideswell & Sons Ltd of Kingsley near Stoke-on-Trent were noted for their impressive fleet of AECs which they kept running until the late 'sixties. The Tideswell brothers have a great personal enthusiasm for AECs and have restored a number of early models in their fleet colours. This fine Mk III dates from 1950 and was still giving stalwart service on long distance work when photographed at Kingsley in 1966.

Probably one of the last Jennings V-cabbed ERF eight wheelers to go into service, this 6.8 dates from 1954. It was based at Whetley Rocks near Stoke-on-Trent and was photographed in 1966 on the East Lancs Road on the outskirts of Liverpool.

One of the largest and best known transport companies around Stoke-on-Trent is Bassetts Roadways of Tittensor whose predominantly Foden fleet aroused great interest among enthusiasts over the years. They operated some magnificent FG eight wheeler and trailer outfits in the 'fifties. At the lighter end the fleet included the modest four wheel boxvan - represented here in the form of a Leyland CS3 Comet dating from 1960.

Opposite: At the time when this photograph was taken this 1969 ERF LV artic was the most modern of trucks. Gardner engines were still the leading choice. Dixons, who were based at Scholar Green, Stoke-on-Trent were regular users of ERFs.

From their base at Tunstall, Stoke-on-Trent, Beresford's
Transport operate a large fleet on general haulage
serving the Potteries and the ceramic tile industry. Their
smart fleet of heavies was painted in the distinctive
style of this Foden until the late 'sixties when their new
grey, green and yellow colour scheme was introduced.
Their fleet once included Sentinel underfloor engined
diesels as well as Fodens and ERFs. This S20-cabbed
dropside six wheeler loaded with grinding pebbles
dates from 1962.

This 1961 Leyland Comet CS3.12R tipper with LAD cab was photographed at a large sand quarry near Leighton Buzzard, the source of high quality silica and foundry moulding sands much in demand by the industrial areas of the West Midlands. This smart truck belonged to Hadley & Cutts Ltd of Wolverhampton.

A centre of interest for the 'sixties truck enthusiast was the Marston Valley Brickworks situated near the M1 motorway at Ridgmont in Bedfordshire. The 'Valley' were renowned for their outstanding fleet of orange trucks lined up in neat ranks within sight of the M1 traffic. AEC Mk III, Foden S18 and ERF KV rigid eights predominated at that time. Marston Valley were taken over by the London Brick Co.

Hamblin's Haulage of Anstey, Leicester, the operators of this 1963 Guy Invincible Mk II, were part of the large Pointer Group whose headquarters were at Norwich. Hamblin also operated a fleet of bulk tippers and heavy haulage outfits for indivisible loads.

Rugby Portland Cement operated this S21 'Mouse' eightlegger seen on the old A5 trunk road. It is a late 1960 model. When first introduced in 1958 the S.21 cab's curvacious shape earned it the nickname 'Sputnik'. Later this much-loved classic was universally dubbed the 'Mickey Mouse'.

K & D, the initials of Kilby & Davison of Bedford, ran a striking fleet of Foden FE6/15 two-stroke eight wheelers on general haulage. Loads frequently included Hemelite products. These handsomely painted vehicles had 'personalised' 555 registration numbers. This 1954 example, NNM555, was photographed near Watford.

Another well known Foden user with specially reserved registration numbers was Direct Transport of Gobowen, near Oswestry in Shropshire. Their blue, cream and red trucks were frequently engaged on steel haulage and were noted for their smart appearance. This splendid 1961 'Micky Mouse' proves that drivers took great pride in their vehicles.

BRS Scunthorpe ran a number of Leyland Octopus flats which were specially equipped to operate with long load 'dollies'. The front of the load rested on a swivelling support set in the body platform. This massive steel shaft was typical of the awkward loads handled by Scunthorpe.

Birmingham is the heart of the motor components industry with countless suppliers of forgings, stampings, castings and presswork. This smart new Bedford KHE 8-tonner with a chromed front bumper belonged to the Bloxwich Lock & Stamping Co and was regularly seen delivering to Vauxhall Motors' Luton factory.

The Automotive Products Co Ltd employed mainly four wheelers to distribute their famous Lockheed clutch and brake components from their factory in Royal Leamington Spa throughout the British automobile and truck industry. This 1959 Dodge, a 3146 model, is also seen delivering to the Vauxhall factory.

Older than its 1965 registration suggests, this re-worked ex-Ministry Leyland Hippo dates from the 'fifties. A considerable number of these ruggedly built six wheelers found their way into civilian haulage fleets in the 'sixties when the Ministry were auctioning off surplus stock. This particularly well prepared example belonged to haulage contractors E & J Davis of Stockwell Road, Birmingham and was mainly employed on transporting iron castings.

Forerunner of the popular Michelotti-cabbed Scammell Routeman II was this less common R8 Routeman I which was in production from 1960 to 1962. It too had a fibreglass cab sharing most panels with the Handyman tractor of the period. A choice of Leyland or Gardner engines was offered coupled to Scammell's traditional 6-speed constant mesh gate change gearbox. Joseph Lucas Ltd operated this 1961 dropside on the distribution of their automotive electrical components.

This Atkinson had already served a 12 year term of work when seen in Dunstable loaded with cylinder block castings from the Midlands in 1964. From BRS in Birmingham this L1586 dropside symbolises British lorries at their peak.

A 1958 Atkinson L2486 tipper belonging to Henry Joyner Ltd of Short Heath Road, Erdington, heads south along the dock road in Liverpool. Joyner's also operated the rarer Sentinel diesels in their fleet of approximately 60 trucks.

On close inspection this Maudslay six wheeler, of 1946 vintage is not the standard 'Maharajah' type but a 'Mogul' four wheeler with a third axle conversion. Power unit was the AEC 7.7 litre diesel. The vehicle, from the fleet of K C Grainger, Wednesfield was photographed while parked up on the A5 'Watling Street' trunk road at Dunstable in 1963.

A 1961 Leyland 19.H/1 Hippo from the large fleet of Edgar Vaughan & Co Ltd, Birmingham. This 12-ton payload six wheeler was engaged on distributing cutting fluids and industrial oils for this well known company.

In the Blackpool region of Lancashire the pale green eight wheeled tippers of Keirby & Perry Ltd were once a common sight. Their varied fleet included an impressive array of old Fodens and Leylands which were gradually phased out when the company was taken over by Kingston Minerals. This 22.O/3 Octopus, a true veteran from 1949, is seen filling up with derv at their Poulton-le-Fylde premises.

Opposite: One of the largest and best known of North Wales hauliers is Williams Bros (Wales) Ltd whose yard at Queensferry, Flintshire housed a fascinating assortment of AEC and Atkinson eight wheel tippers in the 'sixties. This 1956 S1586 on its 40x8 tyres is a typical example. Williams Bros are members of the Transport Development Group. Their fleet also included Dodge and Bedford platform vehicles.

The North West

Many of Britain's best known haulage companies originated in the North West, putting the area in a class of its own when it comes to trucks. As well as including the busy cities of Liverpool and Manchester, it covers the northern half of Wales and extends to the Pennines where it borders with Yorkshire, and northwards to cover most of Lancashire up as far as the top of Morecambe Bay. The South Western edge reaches into part of North West Derbyshire including Buxton and Glossop.

To any devotee of road transport the whole area abounded with interest. But there is one place in the north west that is unbeatable for trucks, and that is Liverpool.

One the oldest seaports, Liverpool once had seven miles of dock road where one could spend days soaking up the unique atmosphere. Quite apart from the local transport firms there would be trucks from all parts of the country, from Scotland to the South Coast. It was, and to some extent, still is, a transport wonderland where lorries unloaded in granite-paved side streets between tall smoke-blackened warehouses. Feed mills, flour mills and transit sheds formed a dramatic backdrop against which the liveried trucks seemed to be perfectly at home.

The orange painted Fodens and AECs of the Liverpool Warehousing Co, members of the Transport Development Group, were a vital part of the scene. Then there were the highly colourful green, blue and red eight wheelers of the Liverpool Cartage Co.

Jarvis Robinson Transport from Bootle daily travelled the dock road with their red Foden and Leyland tractor and trailer outfits carrying portable Guinness Export tanks and other assorted loads. Michael McKenna ran smart maroon Fodens and AECs with a regular South Wales trunk service, as well as a cream coloured fleet on contract to Kraft Foods.

Liverpool was the best place on earth to see maximum capac-

ity rigid eight drawbar outfits from firms like Edward Derbyshire, Anthony Curran, Walter Southworth, George Davies and McCready Brothers, all of whom majored on mid 'fifties Leyland Octopus models.

On the own account front there was, once again, a vast array of famous names including Tate & Lyle, Ranks Flour, Northshore Mills, Bibby's and Jacob's Biscuits. Another regular sight along the dock road were the magnificent blue Foden tankers of A S Jones.

Manchester was also rich in trucks especially around the dock areas and Trafford Park. Among the notable Manchester haulage fleets are William Nuttall whose main customer was Electric Power Storage - the battery manufacturers, Lloyds Transport and Warehousing, tanker firm J M Horrocks of Miles Platting who boasted a fascinating fleet of brown vintage Fodens, Ancliffe (BLT) Ltd who were part of the United Transport group, and Barber Turnock with their Albion CX rigid eights from Stockport.

Giants of the British transport scene, Sutton and Son (St Helens) Ltd, Holt Lane Transport (Whiston) Ltd and W H Bowker Ltd of Blackburn, all had their bases in the North West area. Holt Lane, who were famous for their large fleet of Atkinson eight wheelers and trailers, closed down in 1986 marking the end of an era for old style trailer outfits.

Another fleet which deserves mention was that of Sealand District Transport, subsidiary company of the large John Summers Steelworks at Shotton, Dees-side. They ran a large number of early 'fifties Leyland Octopus dropside lorries, all on 40x8 tyres. These hard worked veterans in their smart livery of maroon and red were often deceptively modern looking, as many were re-cabbed in their lifetime.

Besides being one of the best areas for working trucks, the North West was home to most leading heavy vehicle manufacturers including Leyland, Foden, ERF, Atkinson and Seddon.

Regular visitors to Vauxhall Motors steel stores were the Leyland Octopuses of British Road Services Queensferry depot in North Wales. They operated mainly out of the John Summers works transporting sheet steel.

W H Bowker of Blackburn boasts one of the finest fleets of long distance trucks in the country. They once ran a mixture of Atkinson, Leyland, ERF and Guy rigids and were moving over to artics in the early 'sixties. This Gardner 150-powered Atkinson T746X artic was photographed in falling sleet on a stormy day near Pier Head, Liverpool in March 1964.

John Summers steel works at Shotton, Deeside operated a transport subsidiary called Sealand District Transport, an exclusively Leyland fleet, until the late 'sixties when Fodens and Guy Big J artics were added. Their distinctive maroon Octopus dropsides were most impressive and many of them were older than they first appeared having been re-cabbed during their long operating life. This one is typical being an oil-braked 22.O/1 dating from 1949. All were shod on 40x8 tyres.

Renowned for their practice of 'customising', Dee Valley Transport from Llangollen took a great pride in their vehicles. Most of their mixed fleet of Foden, Sentinel & Guy Rigids were resplendent with bright wheel trims and air horns and they all carried fleet names like 'Lily of the Valley' and 'Queen of the Valley'. This Foden S20 from 1959 was loaded with bagged Fullers Earth products at Redhill in 1964. Its fleet name - 'Pride of the Vale'.

Framed in the rich textures of industrial Manchester this superb Albion CX7N is an early 'fifties model. It carries the fleet name 'Southern Cross' and worked on general haulage with James Spencer of Darwin Street, near Old Trafford.

Sam Longson is a name recently re-introduced after their Chapel-en-le-Frith fleet had been operating under the name of Hanson for many years. This 1963 S24-cabbed Foden in the original Sam Longson livery is seen leaving the Wallerscote plant of ICI Ltd.

Liverpool Docks in the 'sixties was a happy hunting ground for anyone interested in old trucks. This elderly 19.H/1 Leyland Hippo of Jacobs Biscuits had been pounding the Liverpool streets for a good 17 years when this shot was taken in 1966.

One of the many famous makes to be swallowed up into the British Leyland organisation was Maudslay. This 1950 Meritor eight wheeler was among the last operational Maudslays in the country and was one of three still running with TDG member William Harper of Liverpool in the mid 'sixties. It was powered by an AEC 9.6 litre diesel.

Photographed at the Westhoughton yard of Joseph Roscoe this Foden FG6/15 has all the characteristics of the classic 'fifties haulage lorry. With its 40x8 tyres and traditional livery it recalls a lost era in British transport. Dating from 1951 it was employed on long distance trunking to the north and Scotland until the late 'sixties.

This 1949 Vulcan 6PF tipper was used by the Mersey Docks and Harbour Board on work around the huge port of Liverpool and was photographed parked near Pier Head in 1965. It was powered by a Perkins P6, 70bhp diesel.

Long distance hauliers Miller & Gordon were the operators of this 1963 Foden S20-cabbed artic. Their impressive Fodens, Maudslays and AECs were a regular sight on the old A5 trunk route frequently carrying reels of cable from BICC at Prescot. Miller & Gordon were based at Little Woolton Street, Liverpool and were eventually absorbed into the Greenwoods Transport Group of St Ives in Huntingdonshire.

Seafield's 1948 AEC Mandator trailer outfit soldiered on throughout the 'sixties on local work in and around Liverpool's dockland. It survived the trauma of Plating & Testing and carried on giving stalwart service into the early 'seventies.

Welsh granite chippings from Corwen was the regular cargo of this 1956 Leyland ECOS2.5R Comet tipper of the Craiglelo Granite Co in whose Gwyddelwern Quarry this photograph was taken in 1966. Other vehicles in the fleet at the time included early Foden DG models. The Comet with its two-speed axle and O.350 diesel had a creditable top speed of around 60 mph (100 km/hr) which was fast for the 'fifties.

Atkinsons are seen to have a special charisma and Holt Lane Transport's had more than most. Coming from Prescot on the outskirts of Liverpool, these old style eight wheeler and trailer outfits belonged to a fast disappearing breed. They usually carried BICC cable or goods used in cable manufacture. This one is a Gardner 150-powered L2486X registered in 1967. Holt Lane closed down in 1986 - sad news for many haulage enthusiasts.

What made the 'sixties so interesting for the truck enthusiast was the variety of makes still to be seen prior to the 'culling' effect of Plating & Testing. This Sentinel DV4/4 was one of a fleet operated by Wilsons Brewery in Manchester. Dating from 1955 it features the coachbuilt cab and Gardner 5HLW underfloor diesel which were a Wilson trademark. Sentinels were built at the Shrewsbury works now the Perkins engine plant.

Overlooking the grand brick viaduct at Widnes this scene captures some of the unique atmosphere of 'sixties road haulage in the industrial North West. A lone Leyland Beaver and trailer of Runcorn Transport Services trundles slowly towards the A561 through a scene steeped in character. In the far distance on the right of the picture a steam hauled goods train heads towards Ditton junction.

One of the less common rigid eight wheelers was the Seddon DD8 built from 1958 to 1962. This was one of three latex tankers operated by British Vita from their Middleton plant. They were powered by Gardner 6LX diesels and had a design weight of 28 tons in anticipation of higher legal limits. When 28 tons was finally allowed in 1964 it demanded an extra long axle spread of at least 26ft (7.9m) causing difficulty in manoeuvring. This 17ft 9in (5.4m) wheelbase DD8 would not have complied.

The grand era of British haulage is indelibly recorded in this scene along Regent Road, Bootle in 1966. This archetypal wagon and drag on the worn granite setts of the dock road captures the very soul of a bygone era. The Scammell dates from 1956. Note the single 13.50x16 balloon tyres on the third and fourth axles whilst the front and trailer axles have normal 9.00x20s.

The maximum weight, maximum length trailer outfits of H B & H, Newton Le Willows were something of a transport legend in the 'sixties. They operated the dolly and semi-trailer type combination which was the subject of controversy at one time as they were considered to be two 'trailers' in one and therefore not permissible - a theory eventually dismissed. This strik-

ing outfit is hauled by a 1963 O.680 'Power Plus' Octopus. The benefit of using drawbar trailers with eight wheelers vanished when the 'solo' gvw was raised to 28 and eventually to 30 tons. Meanwhile the legal gross train weight limit has remained at 32 tons.

Twenty five years is no mean life for a working truck. This 1939 ERF CI5 had earned its keep twice over and was still going strong in 1964! It served in the fleet of Preston Farmers and was a credit to the quality engineering of ERF Ltd.

The trunk route from London to the North West was frequented day and night by the lorries of Sutton & Son (St Helens) Ltd. Few fleets have captured the imagination as they have, with their superb red Atkinsons, often loaded high with glass containers. This 1956 TS1066 'Chinese Six' was photographed near their Liverpool Road depot in North London.

Having just unhitched its drawbar trailer loaded with Guinness Export tanks this 1947 Foden DG ballast tractor of Jarvis Robinson Transport pauses on the granite setts outside the Guinness warehouse until the next trailer is ready to go back to the docks.

Thanks to S Harrison & Sons of Sheffield, Scammell Rigid Eights could be seen in operation long after their normal life span was up. XS6572 was one of a number purchased from BRS. Originally it operated with Youngs Express Deliveries of Paisley. When this photograph was taken it had been re-engined with a Gardner 6LX.

Opposite: Bulk liquid operations in South Yorkshire were dominated by two large fleets - Harold Wood of Heckmondwike and Smith & Robinson from Rothwell. Both standardised on AECs. Harold Wood also owned AEC dealerships together with Spen Coachbuilders who built most of the cabs on this well known fleet of tankers.

Yorkshire

Until 1972 Yorkshire held the distinction of being the largest county in Great Britain with an area of 6123 square miles (15859 km²) stretching from Humberside to Tees-side. It also has the distinction of constituting a Traffic Area in itself. The area takes in part of North East Derbyshire including Alfreton, Chesterfield and Matlock. Its northern and western extremities do in fact fall within the Northern Traffic Area including Middlesbrough, Northallerton and Sedburgh.

The biggest concentration of transport companies is in the south where some of Britain's greatest industrial cities are to be found, namely Leeds, Bradford and Sheffield. Iron, steel, coal, chemicals, heavy engineering, wool and textiles are the main industries.

As in South Wales there are countless trucks employed in the steel industry centred on Sheffield and Rotherham. For the lorry addict a trip through the smoke blackened townscape in the 'sixties was an enjoyable experience. There were many old-timers still in daily use. Leonard Green's ERF fleet, were regularly seen around the Park Gate Steel Works.

Steel Peech & Tozer's works - the world's largest electric steel plant, was another interesting place where one could get one's fill of BRS Leylands, including their bulk limestone transporters in the bright yellow SPT contract livery. But taking centre stage were the Scammells of S Harrison & Sons Ltd. Their renowned fleet of red Rigid Eights were a landmark on the Sheffield scene.

At Thurgoland on the A629 between Sheffield and Huddersfield stands the premises of Ernest Thorpe Co Ltd who operated a most impressive fleet of green Atkinsons. In Huddersfield itself were the headquarters of Hanson Haulage Ltd, one of the legendary names in road transport. A short distance away up the A642 at Wakefield was yet another large fleet, namely that of F Crowther. Wakefield was also the base of R Hanson & Sons Ltd whose famous fleet of green Atkinson tippers was housed at Newmillerdam.

Fourteen miles or so north west of Wakefield is Bradford, famous as the centre of the wool trade. Among the hauliers who ran the distinctive eight wheelers with wool rack extensions over the cab were James C Ashworth Ltd of Allerton, Henry Long (Manningham) Ltd and J. G. Fielder (Haulage) Ltd. The first two were noted for their AEC Mammoth Majors with 40x8 tyres, the third for their mixed fleet of Leyland and ERF eight wheelers and Thames Traders with third axles.

In Leeds the big haulage fleets include Archbold's (Freightage) and A-One Transport in Jack Lane, Yardley Transport Ltd of Buslingthorpe, Castle Bros at Lowfield Road and T W Nightingale at Ninelands Lane, Garforth on the eastern outskirts.

Two large bulk liquid operations were based in the area - Harold Wood & Sons Ltd of Heckmondwike and Smith & Robinson of Oulton Lane, Rothwell. Both operated AEC rigid eight wheeled tankers. S & R became part of the Hargreaves Group in the early 'sixties but retained their old colours until the late 'sixties when they adopted the Group livery. Harold Wood lost their links with AEC when they were bought by the Tankfreight Division of NFC in the mid 'sixties and took on a new image.

Another large group is Ackworth Transport Co Ltd with its headquarters at Ackworth near Pontefract. They include Onward Transport, Wheeler Road Transport and Harrisons of Dewsbury.

A visit to the east coast would yield other interesting fleets. In Hull were Arrow Bulk Carriers with their yellow Foden and Atkinson tankers. The AECs of Richardson (Hull) Transport Co, were based at Pickering Road.

Many others, unfortunately, must go unmentioned but at least a few well known firms are featured in pictures on the coming pages.

Leeds based A-One Transport were the owners of this 1961 AEC Mk V flat which was specially equipped to transport long beams and girders. The rear end of the load was supported on a single axle dolly, in this case apparently made from the remains of an old Albion. The outfit was seen parked up at Newark-on-Trent in 1964.

In contrast to the more glamorous long distance trucks seen plying the A1 trunk route, this 6-ton payload Seddon Mk5L was used on local distribution by the Brightside and Carbrook Co-op in and around Sheffield. Presumably night time operation was out of the question as its headlamps were missing! The owners had a 200-strong fleet of vehicles.

The steelworks around Sheffield and Rotherham provided much of the traffic for British Road Services vehicles. In the foreground stands a 1957 Leyland 24.O/4 Octopus whilst in the background are two 'LAD' Octopus bulk limestone trucks in the yellow and black contract livery of Steel Peech & Tozer, dating from 1962.

Albion Chieftain FT37L flats lined up at the Sheffield Branch of British Road Services. These 5/6 tonners date from 1956 and were used on general haulage in the South Yorkshire district. They were powered by the EN286 4.88 litre, 4-cylinder diesel developing 75 bhp.

Park Gate Steel at Sheffield were the regular customers for this 1950 ERF of Leonard Green Transport. It was finished in an attractive cream, green and red livery characteristic of a style peculiar to South Yorkshire.

The use of drawbar trailers declined when artics became popular in the 'sixties. One drawback of the trailer outfit was the requirement for a second man or 'statutory attendant'. When seen in 1965 on the A1 this vintage style 1960 Leyland Hippo and trailer was already looked upon as rare.

In the heart of Sheffield's steel making region this 16.S/3 Steer had just off-loaded at Tinsley Wire Industries and was heading back to its Cudworth depot. The vehicle, designed for a 10-ton payload, was operated by well known hauliers Myatt's Transport. The registration suggests that it might be much older than it appears - possibly a late 'forties model which has been re-cabbed.

The green Atkinson eight wheeled tippers of R Hanson could be seen all over the region. This 1964 model was photographed on a miserable day in the centre of Barnsley. It was one of 50 or so similar rigid eights employed on coal haulage from the pits around South Yorkshire. Hanson's were part of the Thomas Tilling Group in the 'sixties.

Perhaps best known for their long distance eight wheeler and trailer outfits which regularly trunked from Dewsbury to London, Harrisons also operated a collection and delivery service in South Yorkshire. The vehicle shown is a nicely liveried Albion FT37L Chieftain of 1955 powered by a 4- cylinder diesel.

Survivor of the mid 1940's this Leyland 12.I.B 'Interim' Beaver was the forerunner of the 600 series 12.B/1 which first appeared in 1947. Standard power unit was a 7.4 litre diesel. Shorts of Halifax continued to run these grand old timers on wool traffic until the late 'sixties. They were fitted with the heavy War Department cab seen on the old RAF Hippos.

The Stanton and Staveley Chemical Co were the operators of this 1953 Atkinson L1586 captured from a high viewpoint. It was one of a fleet of 20 tankers used to distribute chemical products from the coal industry.

The two large front mounted silencers were a hallmark of the famous TS3 powered Commer tractors of the late 'fifties period. These remarkable 2-strokes which developed 105bhp from a horizontal engine with three pairs of opposing pistons, had an unforgettable sound reminiscent of a rapid firing machine gun backed by the distinctive whine of their Roots type blower. This 12-ton payload artic was operated on long distance work by Richard Petty Transport of Bradford.

Below: A notable feature of the trunk vehicles in the fleet of E Brown, Queensgate Filling Station, Beverley in East Yorkshire was the elaborate headboard depicting an elephant's head. Their slogan proclaimed 'Hull and London Nightly Trunk Service'.

W T Flather Ltd of Sheffield used a superb fleet of Foden FG6/15 rigid eights on their regular traffic delivering steel bars. Many of these vehicles were secondhand, ex Cement Marketing Co easily recognisable by their registration numbers and distinctive headboards.

It could be said that this AEC Mammoth Major Mk III and trailer photographed in the Bradford depot of Henry Long (Manningham) Ltd was a dying breed in the late 'sixties. By that time it had served 15 years of hard work carrying capacity loads over the Pennines between South Yorkshire and Merseyside.

One noteworthy operator of maximum capacity trailer outfits was Harrisons of Dewsbury, near Leeds. Their commitment to the type is underlined by the fact that this Ergomatic cabbed Octopus outfit, DHD771E, was added to the fleet as late as 1967 and was put to work on the London trunk. It is depicted when new setting out on its night journey from Harrisons' Westbourne Road depot in North London. Harrisons of Dewsbury were an associate company of Ackworth Transport, Pontefract.

Prior to the fitment of the 'LAD' style cab, Albion Reivers retained their old style coachbuilt type with exposed cast radiator. This 1957 example could have been powered by the 4-cylinder 85bhp diesel. The Comet O.350 was also available. The Reiver operated on solid fuel distribution with Thomas Black of Sheffield.

NMU, the initials of Northern Motor Utilities, was an old established company re-formed in 1953 after de-nationalisation. Much of their traffic involved the movement of products and raw materials for the Rowntree Co based in York. This Willenhall cabbed ERF 5.4 boxvan dates from 1952.

The extensive fleet of AEC tankers once operated by Smith & Robinson was based at Oulton Lane, Rothwell. Their operations date back to 1929 and they grew into one of the largest specialist bulk liquid fleets in the country. In 1961 with a fleet strength of 200 they were acquired by the Hargreaves Group. PWT138 was a 1955 AEC Mammoth Major Mk III and was photographed in Sheffield when ten years old.

Popular choice with so many long established haulage firms was the slow but very reliable Gardner-powered Atkinson. This one, registered in 1958, belonged to the Browns of Beverley fleet already mentioned on page 93.

An AEC Mammoth Major Mk III rigid eight wheeler of 1955 vintage checks out of Tinsley Wire Industries at Sheffield. The Mk III with its 125bhp, 9.6 litre 6-cylinder AEC oil engine and 5-speed constant mesh gearbox was one of the outstanding successes of Britain's heavy commercial vehicle industry at its peak. Full air braking was standard operating on the first, third and fourth axles. Trowbridge Transport were based at Sheffield and ran a regular trunk service to London and the South East.

Newcastle-on-Tyne is called the capital of the North East and it was also the base for Smiles & Co Ltd with their fleet of Atkinson, ERF and AEC eight wheelers. YTY520 was the best looking Atki on the fleet with its 150 Gardner and wide rad. Their eye-catching slogan 'Smiles for Miles' will live on in transport folklore.

Opposite; This ICI Foden 'Mickey Mouse' eight wheeler is mounted with a liquid carbon dioxide tank and is shod on the traditional 40x8 wheels and tyres widely used in the 'fifties. The vehicle was one of a large fleet of Fodens once operated by the world famous chemical manufacturers who have a plant at Billingham.

The North

From a line between Morecambe Bay and the North Yorkshire Moors, the Northern Traffic Area extends up to the Scottish border. At its southern end it takes in Barrow-in-Furness, Northallerton and Tees-side, the homes of several well known transport companies.

From Barrow-in-Furness the leading hauliers were T Brady & Sons and Athersmith Bros who were eventually bought out by the former. Brady's superb fleet of dark blue Leylands was always well turned out as were the dark red Seddons, Leylands and Atkinsons of Athersmiths. Northallerton is well known as the former base of heavy haulage specialists Sunter Bros, part of the United Transport Group, and Prestons of Potto.

Tees-side with its heavy industry boasted several important transport fleets, including F & F Robinson of Stockton, Tees-side Carriers (1963) Ltd, R Durham & Sons Ltd and T A Bulmer of Middlesbrough who will be remembered for the extraordinary Foden lowline eight wheeler specially built along similar lines to the mobile crane chassis but mounted with a flat body and front bolster for long pipes and girders. This famous machine CXG162C was eventually cut down into a short 4-axle tractor unit and hauled a tandem axle semi on the same type of traffic.

Perhaps the largest concentration of transport firms was centred around Newcastle-on-Tyne, the 'capital of the North East' where one could once enjoy the sight of McPhee's old Atkinsons trundling over the Tyne Bridge against an industrial townscape of outstanding character. Fellow Atkinson users were the distinctive 'Smiles for Miles' company based at Blucher. Other memorable names were Baxters Road Services Ltd, tanker operator R Rankin, Alfred W Ellis (Transport) Ltd and Crow's of Gateshead.

Among the interesting own account trucks of the North East were ICI's tanker fleet which was based at Billingham, near Stockton - on - Tees - largely Foden rigids and Scammell artics. Associated Lead Manufacturers Ltd

whose works are at Wallsend, North Tyneside, ran an impressive ERF fleet including KV-cabbed four and eight wheelers and 'Chinese Six' six wheelers, all with dropside bodies and finished in a smart red and maroon colour scheme.

The Northern area straddles the bleak Pennine mountain range, notorious for its hard winter conditions. Before the M6 was extended to Carlisle, trucks on the old A6 were faced with the long slog over Shap Fell before reaching Penrith and heading on for Carlisle and the Scottish border at Gretna Green. The route is renowned on the one hand for its scenic beauty and on the other for its treacherous winter conditons, in which long queues of trucks have frequently been snowbound for days on end. The six-lane M6 motorway has improved the conditions, alleviating some of the winding uphill sections which caused slow moving convoys to build up.

Another well known firm in the Northern area was J L Ion of Milnthorpe who once ran Maudslay and Guy flats. Also from Milnthorpe were the cream Atkinsons of K Fell & Co. E Nelson and Sons whose Trafalgar Garage premises were close to the Westmorland-Lancashire border in Arnside ran a typical long distance fleet of four, six and eight wheeled flats, mainly of Leyland and AEC manufacture.

Moving further up towards the border there were other interesting fleets, including G A Stamper of Penrith and Robsons Border Transport at Carlisle. Robsons have become one of the best known and most widely discussed truck fleets amongst enthusiasts. As well as having a large and beautifully liveried fleet, they built a good relationship with enthusiasts. Their fleet names, all beginning 'Border', are legendary in enthusiasts' circles and the practice of naming has been carried on in spite of two changes of ownership The company, founded by Stan Robson in the pre-war days and re-established in 1954 after denationalisation, has now adopted a white livery instead of the old cream and maroon.

Associated Lead Manufacturers had a particularly fine fleet of ERFs operating out of the Wallsend works on North Tyneside. This 1959 6.8G with the KV cab was photographed at a wayside cafe on the Great North Road in 1967.

The Fodens of Robsons Border Transport have become a legend in UK transport. They have a special magic which has captured the imagination of so many enthusiasts. The practice of using fleet names adds to their individuality. This S20-cabbed Foden FG6/15 named 'Border Raider' was photographed in Luton in 1965. Although Robsons Border Transport was formed in 1954 after de-nationalisation the origins of the company date back to the 'twenties when Stan Robson began with a Model 'T' Ford truck.

This nicely signwritten Seddon DD8 belonging to Gardner Bros (Langley Moor) Ltd of Framwellgate Moor, Co Durham hauled goods for Durham Chemicals and dates from 1960. Appropriately it took its power from a Gardner 150.

Based at Arnside on the southern tip of Westmorland this Maudslay Mogul of E Nelson & Sons was photographed in Luton having delivered a load to the Vauxhall car factory. Nelson's mixed fleet which included Leyland eight wheelers and an AEC Mustang twin-steer were engaged on general haulage making regular journeys to the south of England. This 7.7 litre engined 7/8 tonner dates from 1948.

This neatly sheeted trailing-axle six wheeler is a 1965 AEC Marshal which was basically a 3-axle version of the famous Mercury. Originally they were powered by the same AEC 'AV470' 7.68 litre diesel engine and had a gvw of 20 tons. Later models grossed 22 tons and had the 154bhp 'AV505' engine.

An LV-cabbed ERF 68GX flat from the general haulage fleet of Redpath Bros, Wooller, Northumberland, who ran a number of impressive eight wheelers with livestock containers. This ERF dates from 1965.

F & F Robinson of Yarm Road, Stockton, were the operators of this Foden S20 'Chinese Six' which was registered in 1957. Robinsons had a large Foden fleet on general haulage and when this shot was taken in 1964 were in the process of changing from their traditional maroon livery to this more modern pale blue, maroon and yellow scheme. Other notable Fodens in the fleet included a number of half-cab artics and a rare 32-ton 'Twin-load' artic.

This fully laden CS3 Leyland Comet artic of T Brady & Sons was seen parked up at the Mayflower Cafe on the A6 near Lancaster. The semi-trailer is of the twin oscillating axle type rarely seen these days. Brady's trucks were noted for their excellent colours of two-tone blue and red with traditional signwriting. This Comet is a 1960 model. Loads frequently included goods from Barrow Steelworks and British Cellophane.

Athersmith Bros of Abbey Road Garage, Barrow-in-Furness had a magnificent fleet of dark red Seddons, Leylands and Atkinsons including many eight wheeler and trailer outfits. This DD8 ranks as one of the most impressive outfits on the road. Dating from 1959 it pulled a Crane 8-ton drawbar trailer and the outfit grossed at 32 tons. Power unit was the Gardner 6LX '150'.

Carrying seven and a half tons of floor tiles, this 1955 Leyland Comet was photographed on the A1, en route from Gateshead to London. It was one of four operated by the Armstrong Cork Company on twice-weekly runs to their London depot. They backloaded raw materials, usually cement from West Thurrock or bagged sand from Leighton Buzzard.

Among the less common medium weight trucks were the Seddon '7-tonners' which were built during the late 'fifties by Seddon Diesel Vehicles at Oldham, Lancs. Powered by the Leyland O.350 'Comet' diesel these trucks offered a quality-built alternative to the operator of mass-produced trucks. This 1960 example, a tipper, was operated by Peart Bros of Chester-le-Street. From 1962 the '7-tonners' were powered by the Perkins 6.354.

One of several well known Atkinson operators from the North East was Dents Transport of Tudhoe Colliery, Spennymoor. They operated a regular London trunk service as well as services to Glasgow and Birmingham. This L2486 with dropside body dates from 1958.

Towards the latter 'sixties Robsons Border Transport had moved entirely away from rigid eights and on to the larger capacity articulated outfits but they still remained faithful to Fodens for many years. Lighter vehicles on the Robson fleet were mainly Fords. This Foden S36 named 'Border Marquis' was photographed heading south on the M1 motorway.

The Great North Road is the setting for this impressive 1955 S18 Foden eight wheeled bulker from the fleet of Econofreight, Stockton-on-Tees.

A Cumberland registered Albion Chieftain livestock truck reaches the summit of Shap on the A6, in the days before the M6 was built by-passing this demanding route which once formed the main artery from England to Scotland. Severe winter weather caused perpetual problems for drivers using the route.

Along with many other famous operators of the 'sixties McPhee's, who were based at Newcastle's City Road near the Quayside, have now faded into history. Their dark green fleet of Atkinson and Seddon eight wheelers were part of the Tyneside scene. Nearly all were fitted with 40x8 tyres giving them that special vintage character. Even their later Atkinsons like this 1965 example were so equipped.

This shot shows an old Scammell 'Frameless Eight Wheeler' from the fleet of Imperial Chemical Industries. This chemical tanker dates from 1950 and was based with the Billingham division near Stockton-on-Tees.

Few liveries can compare with that of Pollock (Musselburgh) Ltd. Their fleet outshines all others. This Rolls Royce powered rear-steer Atkinson Silver Knight is representative of Pollock's finest trucks. They all featured fleet names proudly displayed on a tartan sash. KWS666F, new in January 1968, was christened 'Untouchable'. Pollocks operated long distance general haulage services all over the country.

Opposite: Andrew Wishart & Sons Ltd operated a mixed fleet of about 60 trucks based at Institution Street, Dysart near Kirkcaldy, transporting linoleum for Nairn Floorings. They operated in conjunction with A C Horton of Dudley Port, Tipton, Staffs, part of the same group. The fleet was finished in the inimitable Scottish style but this 'LAD' Octopus was especially well turned out with coach style wheel trims all round.

Scotland

Few can rival the Scots when it comes to trucks. Operators 'north of the border' are renowned for their excellent paint jobs. Its a style that others have tried to imitate but the splendour of Scottish liveries is hard to match.

Scotland is home to some of the most famous haulage fleets in Britain. One region is particularly rewarding to the enthusiast - that which stretches from the Forth to the Clyde and from Falkirk down to Clydesdale. In the 'sixties such legendary names as Russell of Bathgate, J & A Smith of Maddiston, Pollock (Musselburgh) Ltd, Forth Road Services Ltd, Sam Anderson of Newhouse, McKelvie & Co and Intercity Transport & Trading Co were all contained within a circle of 10 miles radius.

Having listed such a galaxy of big names the list is still unfinished - Peter McCallum of Airdrie, Hunter's of Airdrie, William Nichol of Coatbridge, D M Smith of Wishaw, James K Allan Ltd of Newarthill, Hugh Harper & Sons Ltd, Whitburn and P Tennant of Forth were also within that 'magic circle'.

A mere stone's throw away were yet more noteworthy fleets. To the east was William Dobson's headquarters at Dorset Place, Edinburgh, and Saddler's Transport in Leith. To the west, Glasgow yielded more big name operators including James Hemphill Ltd, John Barrie (Contractor) Ltd, Isaac Barrie (Transport) Ltd, John Smillie of Govan, John Smith (Whiteinch) Ltd and W H Malcolm of Johnstone near Paisley. By no means is this list complete, but it says more than enough to illustrate the scale of transport operations in the area. All the firms mentioned, most of whom are still operational, boasted superb fleets of nicely liveried trucks.

As if such a feast of heavy metal could leave room for more, a trip over the new Forth Road Bridge opened in 1964 would bring you to more transport-rich territory where Dysart, Dunfermline and Cowdenbeath were the bases of Andrew Wishart & Sons, David West & Son Ltd and Walker Bros (Cowdenbeath) Ltd. Dundee and Aberdeen were the icing on the enthusiasts' cake with Allison's Transport (Contracts) Ltd - later renamed Allison's Freightlines, Andrew Scott & Sons of Tealing, Charles Alexander & Partners Ltd, Munro's Transport (Aberdeen) Ltd, the Shore Porters Society, Gibbs of Fraserburgh and T & M Catto. Largest of the Aberdeen operators was Charles Alexander & Partners, which, after re-forming in 1954 when road transport was denationalised, built up a large fleet and absorbed a number of other established companies. These included John Rhind who ran some impressive Leyland Octopus flats in their 40-strong fleet. Alexander's also had a major holding in Sutherlands of Peterhead and James Paterson & Co (Motor Hirers) Ltd of Aberdeen. Leylands and AECs predominated in the combined fleets.

The northern part of Scotland is more sparsely populated when it comes to trucks. Perhaps the largest of firms in the 'north' was Highland Haulage, which was based at Inverness.

Returning south once more to Ayrshire one would find D McKinnon (Transport) Ltd, who were part of the Tayforth Group, at Kilmarnock. Also at Kilmarnock were Fulton & Semple and McCall & Greenshields.

Not surprisingly the Glasgow-built Albions were widely used in their home country but their role in long distance transport declined when, under British Leyland, they ceased building 'maximum capacity' trucks from about 1960.

The only other Scottish manufacturer in recent times (apart from Volvo) was the Argyle Motor Manufacturing Co Ltd based at East Kilbride in Lanarkshire. They built a number of 16-ton gvw four wheelers in the early 'seventies under the name 'Christina'.

J & R Wright (Haulage) Ltd of Rutherglen and Griffiths of Armadale were among the operators of 'Christinas'.

Though far from comprehensive the following pictorial round up will hopefully recall some of the flavour of Scottish haulage in the 'sixties.

Another example of the Scottish signwriter's skill is the magnificent livery of Anderson's of Newhouse AECs. Sam Anderson's fleet of Mk III eight wheelers were employed on general haulage throughout Great Britain. Their eight wheeled tippers on local work were equally well turned out. The present day Anderson trucks, mainly Scanias, still carry the distinctive signwriting and their traditional slogan 'For Reliable Haulage'.

The 'tin front' L2486 of the early 'sixties was a relatively rare breed of Atkinson aimed to follow the period trend in modern styling. However, the traditional frontal treatment of the exposed radiator outlived such deviations, even to the end of Mk 2 production in 1975. Operating from Wishaw, this smart eight wheeler dates from 1962.

Believed to be the oldest transport company on record The Shore Porters' Society of Aberdeen began with man-handled loads and 'sting' lifts (poles supported on the shoulders of the workmen, who were known as 'pynours', with the goods suspended on ropes) way back in 1498. They progressed to horses in the 1600's and to horse-drawn vehicles in the 1800's. Their origins pre-date Pickfords by 150 years. This Leyland Comet CS3 pantechnicon represents the Shore Porters' fleet in the 'sixties and was photographed at its home base of Aberdeen.

Photographed whilst waiting to take on a load of sawn timber at Kirkcaldy Harbour this beautifully painted Dodge was from the fleet of West's Transport, Dunfermline. It is a 1962 D308 model powered by a Perkins 6.354 diesel.

Long distance hauliers James Kemp (Leslie) Ltd from Croftouterly were the operators of this smart AEC Mercury artic with 26ft (7.9m) semi-trailer. Registered in 1964 it was photographed near the newly opened Forth Road Bridge. It carries fleet name 'The Tyneside Scot' whilst sister vehicle 6205FG 'Thane O'Fife', a 1963 Mercury, stands alongside.

The tradition of using ERF trucks in William Younger's Scottish Breweries fleet was carried on with Scottish and Newcastle. This early LV-cabbed eight wheeler is a fine example from the Edinburgh-based brewery and was photographed in 1964.

Later additions to the well known Allison's fleet from Dundee, Angus, included Guy 'Big J8s'. This one has a Gardner 6LXB '180' engine. Guy offered a wide choice of power units including AEC, Cummins, Gardner, Leyland and Rolls Royce in their 'Big J' rigids. Formerly known as Allison's Transport (Contracts) Ltd the company name was changed to Allison's Freightlines around 1967. Together with James Kemp of Leslie & Spinks Transport, Allisons were part of a group called Amalgamated Transport. This 1968 'Big J' was waiting to off-load steel at Vauxhall Motors, Luton, when it was photographed new. Allison's had a contract carrying steel from Colvilles, Glasgow.

This scene at the Aberdeen premises of Charles Alexander & Partners (Tranport) Ltd depicts two Leyland 'Power Plus' Octopus livestock wagons. Alexander's are the largest hauliers in the area, having absorbed many other sizeable fleets during the 'fifties. They operated long distance services including the transport of fish in refrigerated containers. Close examination of the right hand Octopus in this picture reveals that it has an Albion nameplate - possibly a hint of national pride?

Advertising 'Group 6 Nuts' at '10/- a cwt' (50p for 50kg)
this elderly Atkinson L745 was used by coal merchant
A McDonald to distribute house coal in Glasgow in the
early 'sixties. It was based at Stobcross Station.

A 1956 Leyland 16.S/1 Steer of TDG members' Inter City
Transport & Trading Co Ltd, Cumbernauld
photographed in the outskirts of Edinburgh. This well
known long distance operator has nationwide coverage
with depots in the 'sixties at Glasgow, Edinburgh,
Manchester, Bolton, Derby, Brierley Hill and St. Albans.

Seen parked up at Perth some 80 miles south of its home base at Aberdeen, this 'Power Plus' Leyland Octopus is a fine example from the fleet of John Rhind Transport Ltd who belonged to Charles Alexander & Partners.

Scottish eight wheeler from the 'fifties. A Glasgow-built Albion 'HD57L' operated by paper manufacturers Alex. Cowan & Co Ltd of Valleyfield Mills, Penicuik, who became part of Reed International. Dating from 1952 it was built of Albion components throughout. Leyland took over the Albion concern in 1951 and finally closed it down in 1987 marking the end for one of the most famous truck makers. Vehicle production ceased as long ago as 1980 and the last Albion-badged trucks as long ago as 1971.

There are few transport companies more widely known than J & A Smith of Maddiston who in the mid 'sixties had a fleet of around 375. From their formation in 1933 the company, under the directorship of brothers James and Alexander Smith grew to absorb several other hauliers, among them H L Walker of Thornaby-on-Tees, A & E Morris of Birmingham and Alexander Scott (Contractors) of Glasgow. A nation-wide network of depots was established. In 1968 they joined the United Transport Group. J & A Smith were noted for their smart livery of cream, maroon and red in which this 1956 Octopus appears. Most of their trucks had illuminated headboards reading 'Smith for Service'.

Another fine example from the Andrew Wishart fleet referred to on page 112 was this 1955 Foden FE4/8 photographed at their Dysart depot in 1967.

Fleet names were especially popular amongst Scottish operators. A noteworthy example is that of Daniel Stewart's smart Ergomatic AEC Mandator reefer - 'Oor Wullie', seen near the Forth Road Bridge in July 1967. A shield depicting a Scottish piper proudly adorns the centre of the grille. This TG4R Mandator must be one of the earliest, the range having only been introduced at the 1964 Earls Court Show.

The inimitable quality of Scottish liveries is plain to see in this fine KV-cabbed ERF 6.8GX dating from 1962. It was resplendent in deep maroon and red with tasteful gold signwriting. It belonged to the 30-strong fleet of Hugh Harper of Whitburn and was photographed in the Grass Market, Edinburgh.

World famous for its many brands of whisky, Scotland is also the home of numerous breweries including that of Tennents based in Glasgow. VSG35 was a 1960 AEC Mk V of a type used to trunk bottled beer to distribution depots. Here it is seen loaded up with crates at Tennents' Edinburgh brewery about to set out on its next trip.

From running Foden rigid eights in the 'fifties and early 'sixties, James Hemphill changed to maximum capacity 32-ton artics on their large bulk liquid tanker fleet which was based at Inglefield Street, Glasgow. This fine example hauled by a 1965 S24-cabbed 'Chinese Six' 2-stroke unit was photographed alongside the A74 on Beattock.

Long service is often associated with heavily-built trucks like ERFs and Atkinsons, but this Bedford OLB 5-tonner wasn't doing so badly after 20 years on the road. The proud owner stands next to the old timer which was seen delivering in Edinburgh in the late 'sixties. It has the '28 hp' Bedford 6-cylinder petrol engine which developed 84bhp.

Michelotti's extraordinary styling on the Scammell Routeman II looks modern even in the 1980s. The design was however launched in 1962 and wore well until the last ones were registered 20 years later. This one, from the fleet of Peter McCallum & Sons Ltd of Airdrie, dates from 1964 and its 40x8 tyres give away something of its vintage. Peter McCallum were members of the Transport Development Group.

One of the largest groups in Scotland was Tayforth, an NFC company, to whom this 1960 Albion Caledonian tanker belonged. Road Services (Forth) was one of six companies in the Group which had 22 depots nationally and boasted over one million square feet of warehousing. Many of the company's tankers operated in contract customers' liveries.

This 'S20' Foden with a special semi-trailer for long loads served in the fleet of McKelvie & Co who were also members of the TDG. It was registered in 1959. McKelvie & Co ran a large fleet of vehicles from their premises at Barrhead, Paisley & Motherwell and were engaged in both general and heavy haulage.

Some of the special flavour of Scottish transport is captured in this shot of a 1958 Albion Reiver belonging to Ed Robertson, Dundee seen passing through the main street of Milnathort, Kinross in 1967.

Indicative of the shift from rigids to artics for long distance haulage, this 1963 AEC Mandator Mk V 24-ton gcw outfit was one of a number of artics to enter the fleet of Munro's Transport Ltd, Aberdeen, in the early 'sixties. This one-time operator of rigid eights used the vehicle on trunk operations to the South East involving round trips in the region of 1000 miles.